Whispers of the Soul

Chandra Brown

BookLeaf Publishing

Presentation by *BookLeaf Publishing*

Web: www.bookleafpub.com

E-mail: info@bookleafpub.com

ISBN: 9789358311280

First edition 2023

This book is dedicated to my Aunty Jody
who is my greatest fan, supporter, and
inspiration. In Lak'Ech!

ACKNOWLEDGEMENT

Thanks to BookLeaf Publishing for this opportunity. Thanks to my friends and family for the space they gave me to create.

For A Split Second

For a split second, I forgot you weren't here
For a split second, I wanted to hold you near
For a split second, I wanted to share
But, then I remembered, you weren't there

Anxiety

Thoughts swirl, crowd my mind
Overthinking, what would they find
Anxiety pours through my very soul
What if I'm not good enough, what if I'm told
Nothing at all, not a single word
Time flies away as the silence unfolds
Paranoia begins, my mind betrays
But, one thing's for sure, no one ever stays

In The Darkness

In the darkness, you found me
In the darkness, I cried
In the darkness, I thought you couldn't see
In the darkness, I fought, I tried
You found me, in the places I would hide
You found me underneath the bed
You found me in the closet, too
You found me everywhere you looked
No one could save me from you

You Weren't There

I cried out for you
But you weren't there
I ran to you
But you weren't there
I reached out to you
But you weren't there
So I stopped hoping
Because you didn't care

Wishing Star

I wished every night
On that same very star
That this will be the day
We will finally depart
From this evil world
That gave us nothing
But heartache and pain
And everything that evil brings

I See You

I see you in the distance
Stern with a frown
Hoping you would see me
Save me before I drown
These tears streaming down
Trying to not let you see
How much I truly need you
How much I need to be free

The Great Beyond

All I ever wanted was for you to hold me
To tell me everything would be alright
To keep me from the darkness
And to carry me through the night
Save me from this nightmare
I can't keep going on
Save me from this evil
Please take me to the great beyond

Monsters

The monsters under my bed
They say it was all in my head
They say not to be scared
It's as if no one bothered or cared
But, the monsters, they are real
Their hands I can feel
The monsters are real, but they're not under my
bed
I silently cry as I hold my breath
The monsters are here, I can feel them close
The monsters are real, they are the ones I trusted
the most

Abandoned

I lift my head to the sky
Praising you through the night
I stand steadfast as long as I try
But, the demons surround me though I put up a
good fight
Where are you, Lord? Please help me, save me
I cry out to you, I beg and plead
You abandoned me, I trusted Thee
But, you left me, to fight alone struggling to be
free

My Final Goodbye

The waves greet me as I stare into the black
abyss
Waiting for that moment when clarity hits
The moon is shining, the stars are bright
I wait for that moment when everything is right
The surf is crashing
My world is collapsing
Yet I know the time is nigh
To say my final goodbye

Sweet Embrace

In the darkness, I found the light
The sun shone through the coldness of the night
You rose from the shadows
You pulled me from below
And now the world I can face
Because of your sweet embrace

Whole again

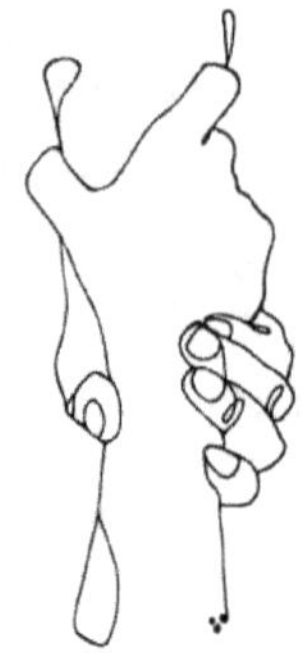

You reached for me
Out of the depths of hell
You caught me
when I stumbled and fell
Battered, broken, bruised
You are the one that I choose
Down to the depths of my soul
It is you who makes me whole

Angel

You give me much-needed space
To deal at my own pace
The demons of my past
The scars that seem to last
You hold me in your sweet embrace
As I heal from the ghosts that I must face
You cover me with unconditional love
You are an angel sent from above

Final Breaths

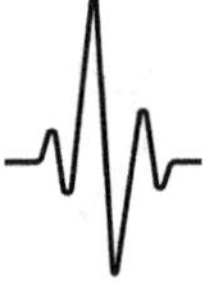

The darkness closes all around me
As I gasp my final breaths
Fear strangles, it grips me
The nearer I approach death
But, in the moment that I surrender
And finally come to a place of peace
My breathing starts to relax
And I find a sense of relief

Rejoice

We talk every day
As I try to come up with things to say
So I can hear your sweet voice
That soothes and brings me joy
It does not matter the words we speak
It's only your tenderness I dare to seek
For it's your love I can hear in your voice
And, it's for that reason, I rejoice

A New Day

As I watch the sun rise
I am reminded of all that I have overcome
To get to this place of peace
To this new person I have become
As the sun rises past the horizon
I can feel the rays' warm embrace
I can feel a new day dawn
My worries disappear without a trace

If I Could Turn Back Time

If I could turn back time
I would tell you that I love you
I would tell you that I care
I would stop the hand that hurt you
I would let my feelings bare
I would hold you in my arms
I would kiss your tender face
If I could turn back time
I would gladly take your place

I Love You

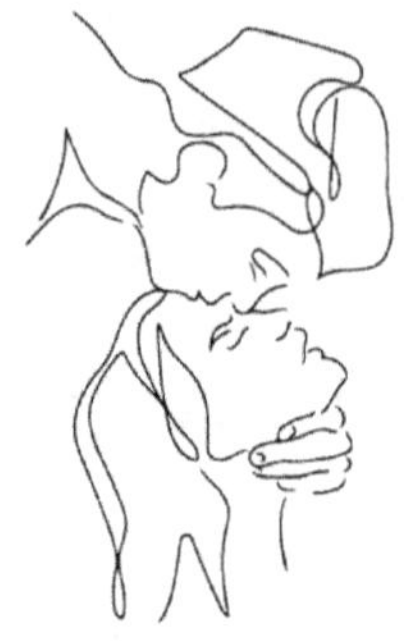

I love you in the morning
I love you in the evening
I love you in the noontime
I love you even when I'm dreaming
I love you when your mood is depressed
I love you in your happiness
I love you til the end of time
I love you for you are mine

I Look To The Heavens

I look to the heavens
In search of your face
I look to the heavens
Hoping to feel your embrace
I look to the heavens
Waiting for a sign
I look to the heavens
Knowing that you will always be mine

Rollercoaster

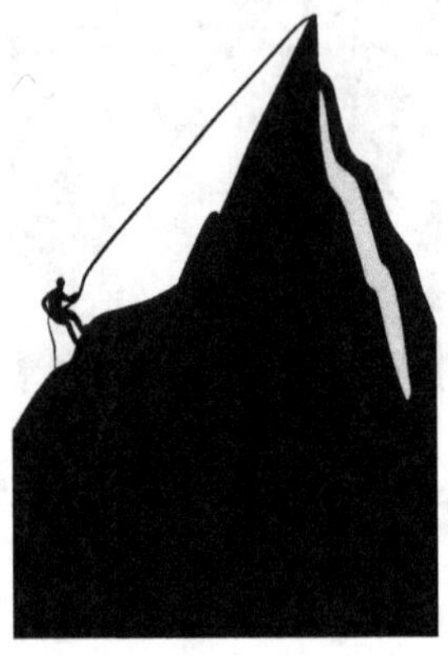

The mountains are high
The valleys are low
Life is a rollercoaster
With its blow after blow
But then you reach the top
And all you can do is smile
Enjoy the victories when you can
And hope that it lasts for a while

In Lak'Ech

From the moment I saw you
I just knew
You were meant for me
And I was meant for you
It was love at first sight
On that beautiful day
I knew we were meant to be
For I took your breath away
We will always be
You and me
Best friends, soul mates
And everything in between
I am forever yours
You are eternally mine
This thing we have together
Is nothing short of divine
You hold me in a tender embrace

Forehead to forehead I melt into your sweet
caress
As I whisper softly in your ear
For only you to hear
The words you first spoke to me
Those sweet words - In Lak'Ech

www.ingramcontent.com/pod-product-compliance
Lightning Source LLC
LaVergne TN
LVHW050507210726
843509LV00015BA/3035